# ICELAND

Iceland
Review

# ICELAND

Iceland is a country of raw and intense beauty. The forces of nature at work on this mountainous North Atlantic island have sculptured a unique landscape. Storms and gales shattered the coastline into countless narrow fjords; lava from still active volcanoes has edged its way across the highland plateaux; mighty glaciers have gouged deep valleys into the face of this geologically scarred, but relatively young land.

These photographs invite you not only to discover the geography of Iceland, but also some of the country's natural phenomena: geothermal springs, thundering waterfalls, spouting geysers and bubbling mud pools. Nature in Iceland is omnipresent. Even in the capital, Reykjavík – its modern skyline dominated by brightly painted apartment buildings and family homes – the austere landscape is still clear to see all around.

Iceland is also a naturalist's paradise. Due to the the country's unspoilt nature and low population density – barely 280,000 people live here – millions of seabirds flock to the country's clifftops and coastal meadows to nest during the bright summer months. In addition, whales, dolphins and seals are to be found in sizable numbers offshore, in some of the cleanest waters anywhere on Earth.

From its towering snow-capped mountains and dusky hills swirling in mists, to its jagged fingers of land jutting into the sea, Iceland never fails to weave a magical spell over all who journey there.

### ◄ ÞINGVELLIR

The most historically significant site in Iceland, Þingvellir (literally 'Assembly Plains'), was selected as the location of the country's first parliament in 930AD and, as such, is the oldest in the world. The rift between the European and North American tectonic plates, upon which Iceland sits, is clearly visible here – an ever widening chasm as the plates slowly pull apart.

### STROKKUR ►

Spouting boiling water 20m in the air roughly every three minutes, Strokkur is one of Iceland's most popular tourist attractions. Close by, big brother Geysir became active again after an earthquake in 2000, and gives its name to every other spouting hot spring in the world.

## Landmannalaugar

An oasis in the surrounding grey lava deserts of the Interior, Landmannalaugar is Iceland's second largest geothermal field. Many of the multi-coloured peaks here are composed of rhyolite, formed by geothermal and volcanic activity.

## Gullfoss ▶

The Gullfoss waterfall (literally 'Golden Falls') derives its name from the rainbows which regularly appear over the rising clouds of spray.

### ◄ VESTMANNAEYJAR

The 'Westmann Islands', off Iceland's south coast, were created by submarine volcanic eruptions up to 10,000 years ago. In 1963, an eruption created the new island of Surtsey. In 1973 a fissure opened near the town of Heimaey, destroying about 40% of its homes, though everyone was evacuated by boat without harm. Today fishing is the principal occupation and some of Iceland's richest fishing grounds lie close to the islands.

### SKÓGAFOSS ►

According to ancient legend, one of Iceland's early Viking settlers hid a chest of treasure at the foot of thundering 60m Skógafoss waterfall. Numerous attempts to find the riches have failed.

## ARNARDRANGUR, REYNISDRANGAR AND DYRHÓLAEY

The distant sea stacks of Reynisdrangar, feature in the view off Iceland's southernmost coast. Close by, the Dyrhólaey rock arch (above) located in an important area for breeding birds, is itself a favourite nesting site for puffins, Arctic terns, guillemots and fulmars.

## Lómagnúpur, Skaftafell and Öræfajökull

No less than 16 different ice-caps converge in the southeast of Iceland
to form Europe's biggest glacier, Vatnajökull. The southern snout of this
ice giant, the spectacular Öræfajökull icecap, rises above the verdant expanses of
the country's spectacular national park, Skaftafell. The highest peak in Iceland,
Hvannadalshnúkur (2119m), protrudes from the glacier, posing a serious
challenge to even the most experienced mountaineer.

## HÖFN AND VATNAJÖKULL

The village of Höfn is dwarfed by the sheer expanse of ice that comprises Iceland's biggest glacier, Vatnajökull. The ice conceals several active volcanoes beneath its surface – during one recent spell of volcanic activity, blocks of ice as large as apartment buildings were dislodged by the eruption.

### JÖKULSÁRLÓN ▶

Jökulsárlón, or the 'Glacial River Lagoon' is one of Iceland's deepest glacial lakes. At 100m deep, the lake allows icebergs that have sheared from the Breiðamerkurjökull glacier to float in its milky blue waters. Although predominantly white in colour, the ice blocks are sometimes scarred black by moraine material from the icecap or tinted blue. Boat trips among these wonders are available in season. If the scenery seems oddly familiar, it was used as a suitably dramatic backdrop in the James Bond film, *A View to a Kill*.

### ◀ SEYÐISFJÖRÐUR, EASTERN FJORDS

After the herring boom of the nineteenth century, Seyðisfjörður, which lies at the head of this fjord, was set to become Iceland's biggest port, but the steep mountains on three of its sides made expansion impossible. Today, however, it remains an active fishing and fish processing centre, with a few elaborately carved timber houses as evidence of past prosperity in its tiny centre. Every Thursday in summer, there is a hive of activity on the dockside when the ferry linking Iceland with mainland Europe arrives.

### ESKIFJÖRÐUR, EASTERN FJORDS

Like so many other villages in Iceland's Eastern Fjords, Eskifjörður owes its prosperity to the sea. It was recognised as a trading centre in the late eighteenth century and economic activity peaked during the herring boom of the following century. Looking across the eponymous fjord, Hólmatindur mountain provides a spectacular backdrop.

### ◄ DETTIFOSS

One of the most breathtaking sights in Iceland. Five hundred cubic metres of water per second from the Jökulsá á Fjöllum river thunder down the waterfall. Spray from Dettifoss can be seen several kilometres away from this spectacular piece of natural engineering.

### HERÐUBREIÐ ►

Its crown-like formation has earned Mount Herðubreið the name 'Queen of the Mountains'. Situated in a lavafield in Iceland's uninhabited Interior, the mountain's symmetrical shape is the result of a sub glacial volcanic eruption. Close by, Herðubreiðarlindir, an area of hot springs and grassland, is literally an oasis in the surrounding desert of grey sand.

◀ Öskjuvatn and Víti, Askja

The route to Askja in the Highlands may be a difficult journey through twists and turns, but it is one worth enduring. Within the crater of the Askja volcano in Iceland's forbidding Interior are two lakes, the deep and wide Öskjuvatn and the smaller Víti – whose name means 'hell'. Early travellers knew it as a devil's cauldron from which all living things would flee. Today though, the view from the crater's rim and a swim in Víti's opaque waters is a memorable experience.

Mud Pool Crater, Námafjall, Mývatn

Bubbling pits of mud and accompanying sulphur vents, generated by geothermal activity under the Earth's surface, lace the air at Námafjall mountain in the northeast of Iceland with noxious gases. The ground around the mud pools is very thin and often discoloured, an indication that the Earth's crust here is very thin and not safe to walk on.

### Hverfjall, Mývatn

The cone of Hverfjall is a landmark of northeast Iceland. It lies close to Lake Mývatn, a popular area of natural beauty, well known for its birdlife and nearby geothermal features.

### Goðafoss ▶

Goðafoss (literally 'Waterfall of the Gods') is named after the pagan chief who hurled his heathen idols into it when realising that Iceland would accept Christianity.

## HVÍTSERKUR IN HÚNAFJÖRÐUR

In Iceland, myths and legends are in no short supply, perhaps nowhere more so than at Hvítserkur in the north of the country, where this 15m-high sea stack is reputed to have once been a troll. Returning home after plundering a nearby monastery, the creature was turned to stone as the first rays of daylight struck its giant figure.

## ÍSAFJÖRÐUR, ÍSAFJARÐARDJÚP, WESTERN FJORDS ▶

The principal town of Iceland's Western Fjords, Ísafjörður, is hemmed in on all sides by tabletop mountains and craggy fjords. During the winter months, the serpentine roads that weave their way around the region's fjord network are often blocked by avalanches. Across the waters of Ísafjarðardjúp bay, the entire stretch of the Snæfjallaströnd coast was once under cultivation. Today, abandoned farmsteads bear witness to the hardship and isolation people who lived here once endured.

◀ LÁTRABJARG, WESTERN FJORDS
The bird cliffs of Látrabjarg form Iceland's
westernmost extremity. Windswept and
rugged, this 12 kilometre-long cliff provides
summer nesting grounds for hundreds of
thousands of seabirds including puffins,
guillemots, razorbills and kittiwakes. The
puffins are a special attraction here, as they
allow people to approach within a few feet.

### RAUÐASANDUR, WESTERN FJORDS

It is not hard to imagine a more remote and dramatic setting for
a murder mystery. Indeed, one of Iceland's well known authors chose
the golden sands and crashing surf of Rauðasandur as the location for a best-selling
novel that dramatised real life tragedies. Now the beach and grazing land is home
to only two farming families and their livestock. This spit of land opening out
into the waters of Breiðafjörður fjord is also known for its seals.

## FLATEY IN BREIÐAFJÖRÐUR

The rich flower meadows and gently shelving shingle coves of the small island of Flatey, in Breiðafjörður fjord, are a favourite destination for holidaymakers. Many of the brightly painted timber houses on the island have been bought and restored by people from the capital. Just two families live on the island all year round.

SNÆFELLSJÖKULL, SNÆFELLSNES ▶

A pyramid of eternal snow and ice, the Snæfellsjökull glacier marks the furthest point of the Snæfellsnes peninsula in western Iceland. A backbone of jagged mountains runs the length of the peninsula, which is named after the snow fell at its tip. Writer, Jules Verne, chose the icecap as the starting point for his *Journey to the Centre of the Earth*. The glacier harbours an active volcano amid its layers of ice, although there have been no recorded eruptions during the time Iceland has been settled.

### Reykjavík

Looking across 'The Pond' to Reykjavík's postmodern City Hall. The Pond is the city's largest body of water and home to over forty species of bird, including year round inhabitants such as the distinctive whooper swan. At New Year, fireworks light up the city and the impressive 70m steeple of Hallgrímkirkja (left), or the 'Church of Hallgrímur', Iceland's most famous religious poet.

### THE PEARL, REYKJAVÍK

Geothermally heated water was once stored in these tanks, to provide Reykjavík with instant hot water. A revolving restaurant, The Pearl, sits on top of the tanks.

### THE BLUE LAGOON ▶

A swim in the ethereal Blue Lagoon is a sublime experience. Its tempting waters remain at an attractive 36-40° all year round and are beneficial to the skin.

# SAILING FROM AKUREYRI, EYJAFJÖRÐUR, ICELAND'S LONGEST FJORD

Design and Production: Colin Baxter Photography Ltd.

Text: James Proctor, © Colin Baxter Photography Ltd.

Photography © Colin Baxter Photography 2001

Printed in Hong Kong

Published in 2001 by Iceland Review ©

ISBN: 9-979-51151-6